Turning Prayers into Love Notes

Widline Pierre

© 2017 by Widline Pierre.

All rights reserved. No part of this book may be reproduced, stored in a retrieval system or transmitted in any form or by any means without the prior written permission of the publishers, except by a reviewer who may quote brief passages in a review to be printed in a newspaper, magazine or journal.

First printing
ISBN: [0692908919]

© 2017 Copyrights by Widline Pierre.
WIDLINE PIERRE PUBLISHING

Printed in the United States of America

Cover Design: Shari Designs, www.sharidesigns.net
Cover Photography: Kerry Ulysse, www.96mm.co
Editors: Marc Laurore & Val Pugh-Love

Praise for Turning Prayers into Love Notes by Widline Pierre

"Widline Pierre is an upstanding friend, very hard worker, and well-driven individual. She is very motivated despite any challenges she faces, and she does not stop until she achieves success in her goals. She has applied all her motivation skills to help others, which has inspired her to write Turning Prayer into Love Notes."

- Ricardo Grant, Owner of 5 Star Fitness Gym

"You might have been struggling in your relationship with God for years, due to the lack of prayers or facing serious obstacles that have prevented you from seeing the glory of God. Well, the right time has come to triumph over your spiritual weaknesses. This book *"Turning Prayers into Love Notes"* is specially written with the purpose of improving your spiritual struggles. After reading this book, it is certain that you will become addicted to prayers and you will never be the same person like before."

- Claudin Estime, Student at Oral Robert University and Superintendent of Sunday School

"Turning Prayers Into Love Notes is truly an inspirational book that every Christian needs to have in their devotional studies. All prayers count. But, what are you praying for? This book will help you stay focused on how to pray to our heavenly father. Amazing!"

- Louis Vildor, educator, entrepreneur and President of iHELP Academy

FOREWORD

I am honored to have been chosen to write the foreword for such an inspirational book. *Turning Prayers into Love Notes* is a bold effort to reach millions with a very unique praying and intercession technique.

As the author of the book, Widline Pierre has devoted her youth to actively practicing the principles and power of prayer. She incorporated her tactics as a prayer warrior to encourage others to pray with a sensible, pure and loving heart. She uses the metaphoric and symbolic definition of marriage as it is applied to Christ and the body of believers known as the church. As Christ is the groom, the church is the bride, Widline is encouraging all believers to pray to God as we are sending love notes to our husbands or wives. As stated in Ephesians 5:25-27 "Husbands, love your wives, as Christ loved the church and gave himself up for her, that he might sanctify her, having cleansed her by the washing of water with the word, so that he might present the church to himself in splendor, without spot or wrinkle or any such thing, that she might be holy and without blemish." Our responsibility as the church/bride is to be faithful to our groom/Jesus Christ by *turning our prayers into love notes*.

While reading this book, we will learn how to choose our words wisely while praying. We will learn to turn our prayer requests to God into love poems. We will learn to make kind love notes of our demands to God. Lastly, we will learn to turn praying sessions into a date with our groom. Turning prayers into love notes will instill a broader perspective of praying strategies to all readers.

Lovely Joubert

CEO, Lovely Joubert Film Productions

PREFACE

"Don't worry that God never listens to you. Worry if you never communicate with Him."

The objective of this book is to provide you an understanding of what it means to turn your prayer into love notes. After years of listening to others, searching, reading, and developing prayer skills, I look around and still see we are weak in the ways we pray. A lot of people like to share their years of experiences in the church, yet some of them still have no idea what prayer is. This book aims to increase spiritual awareness and to improve our communication and prayer skills. This is the perfect time to get everyone's attention and to motivate Christians and non-Christians to truly turn their face to our Creator, God.

Praying to God should be a sense of joy, intimacy, and fulfillment. However, it does not happen to be so because of our approaches. I once lost my motivation to pray because I was not turning my prayer into love notes. Consequently, God was not answering my prayer. I used to pray as I was trying to bribe Him to do things for me. I would say things like: "God, if you do this for me, then I will do that for you."

I have a strong conviction that many of us, if not all, have prayed once or twice like this. The moment I learned to start giving love to God through my prayer, I discovered my spiritual and personal strengths. My low self-esteem turned to full potential, and the experience has been invigorating.

I decided to include a little of my story here to show my great readers that my story is like theirs. I will not rest until I reach a multitude of people for God, and it starts with this book.

I am a young married woman who is trying to inspire a new generation for Jesus Christ. I was a product of a prodigal daughter who once left Jesus Christ, church, and all her beliefs. I did most of my growing years with my grandmother who was and still is so involved in church activities. She used to go to the hospital every Sunday to visit ill people. During her missionary trips, she would bring me along with her while attending many church revivals. As I got older, the love I had for God and church faded away, and I found myself doing things I never imagined doing. Although, a part of me knew what I was doing was wrong - especially being raised in a home with Christian values.

The Lord in His mighty ways allowed me to experience many things I thought were good, which turned out not to be so. Just to name a few things, I experienced going clubbing, piercing my belly not once but twice, and even sex before marriage. I did not know that my body was the temple of God. Caution: I am not a faultless writer, and I want all the young people to know that perfection can only be achieved if you let the Holy Spirit in. God had enough of my nonsense, and He decided to flip the perfect world I thought I was living in upside down. The Lord knew the seeds He had sowed in me were not going to die, so He gave me one choice and one last chance to get my act together and to truly serve Him.

Over the past five years, I have experienced the Holy Spirit in ways I did not think was ever possible. I have developed this great intimacy with Jesus Christ which has given me the inspiration to write this wonderful book. All credits go to my God through His Son Jesus Christ and the Holy Spirit. If you are looking to have a personal discovery with Jesus Christ and a better view of what you can gain when turning your prayer into love notes, then you have found the right book.

ACKNOWLEDGEMENTS

I would like to acknowledge my Lord, Christ Savior, for giving me once again this great inspiration and making everything possible for me. I want to thank everyone who has touched my life in an amazing way as well as those who have touched it negatively. Both ways have helped me to grow and mature.

Thank you to my father, siblings, nieces, and nephews. I am deeply grateful to my lovely mother for her tough love and her hard work raising four headache children in Lake Worth, Florida. A special thank you to my grandmother who used to drive me insane to serve the Lord and for believing in me no matter what I did.

I want to thank my Pastor, Wendell Charles, and his wife First Lady Nicaise. You both are amazing. Thanks to Brother Marc and his wife Benise, Deacon Claudin and Mrs. Carole Emile who have guided, challenged, and inspired me to surrender to God completely. Thanks to all my friends: Celeste, Marie, Rudy, Genie, Carin, Milien, Miller, Mona Jeudy for all your prayers, Lovely for being my co-host for six years, and the members and all the young adults at Church of God Elected. In addition, Kerry - no words, I pray the Lord continues to anoint you.

Elysabeth, girlfriend, you are an amazing woman! Throughout this wonderful journey, I have met and talked to some amazing people and all have been a blessing from God.

A special thank you to Jasira Monique for exercising your God-given talents, abilities, and kindness towards me. Thank you to Dejean (Junior) and Sandra Charite for all the great insightful information and resources.

I am indebted to my husband; you are an exceptional man. A special thank you to you Obson Jacque who always leads by example even in the worst of situations. Your love and support has made it possible for me to stay focused and for this dream to come true.

I have to thank you again, Marc Laurore. A special thank you to you; your dedication to this book has been beyond words. I thank God for the new gift He gives and you are an amazing editor. I also want to thank your family, especially your wife, for allowing you to have all the sleepless nights while editing the book.

I want to acknowledge all of you who will be reading this book and thank you all in advance. I pray that the Holy Spirit can reveal Himself to you all and pour many blessings.

INTRODUCTION

The day I truly got saved, I started thinking: *How am I going to communicate to this powerful God, and what kind of magical words am I going to use?* I have come to realize in my walk with Jesus Christ these past five years that He does not really care about big vocabulary words. Instead, He just wants us to do the will of God as He did. Once I discovered that, I began talking to Him in the same fashion I do when I call my best friend - just in a more powerful way. However, this great inspiration did not come to light until I had a flashback about the first time I thought I was in love. Thinking back to how I used to communicate with this individual, I thought to myself: *What if I talk to God as if He is my lover?* Technically, Jesus Christ is the lover of our souls. Understanding this, I found myself immersed in a deep and profound relationship with God, which made it easier to pray and communicate with Him. I learned to turn prayer into love notes or letters. For instance, I began to use words like: my love, my darling, mon amour in French, and even mi amor in Spanish.

Every day, we talk sweetly to people we care for and love. So why is it hard to show the same affection and passion when we are communicating with God? I do not refer to my conversations with God as prayers; they are love notes. Often, we are nervous or afraid to talk to God because we do not know how to pray. However, you are simply talking to God in a more elevated way than you would normally do with someone you love. In this love note, I have a large collection of poems to help you to start communicating with God through His Son, Jesus Christ. You can use these poems until you have learned to talk to Him using your own words in your own style. It is a great resource that has brought me closer to Jesus Christ. Naturally, I wanted to keep it all to myself. Then, I realized this is not my doing but a gift. For freely I have received, and freely I must give back. I pray and hope this book and the workbook both help you with your relationship with God. I strongly believe this is not just a book, but a mission of building a healthy and stronger relationship with God, Our Father, The Son, Jesus Christ and the Holy Spirit.

CONTENTS

FOREWORD	5
PREFACE	7
ACKNOWLEDGEMENTS	10
INTRODUCTION	12
BEGINNING	19
CHOOSE WORDS THAT SOUND RIGHT	30
PRAYER SKILLS	39
RENDEZVOUS	47
FINEST PRAYER	55
COLLECTIVE POEMS	83
THIS IS CRRAAAZY	99
THE WONDER OF GOD	113
WHAT'S IN PRAYER?	119
THE PROCESS OF INTIMACY	125
ABOUT THE AUTHOR	129
BONUS	130

Turning Prayers into Love Notes

Beginning

"The beginning is extremely important. Believe me, it does matter. At times, it can be very difficult…"

God's beginning is before time as we know it. He told Jeremiah, "Before I formed you in the womb I knew you, before you were born I set you apart; I appointed you as a prophet to the nations" (1:5). Considering this, everything has a beginning, just as it is mentioned in Genesis: "In the beginning, God created the heavens and the earth" (1). Picture the beginning of any relationship - whether with your parents, yourself, your best friend, teachers, your wife, your children, your husband, or co-workers. How was the beginning? Were there any bumps, or was it love at first sight? The beginning is extremely important. Believe me, it does matter. At times, it can be very difficult, just like starting a business, building a home or looking for a career. This book is designed to help you with your experience with Jesus Christ, and I pray you will find it very helpful.

If you've done this already, do you recall the first time you invited God into your life? Recall the first time you said, "I surrender my life to You Lord." Can you recount the rush of emotions that enveloped you? Do you remember the excitement, joy, and peace that hovered over you? Since I grew up in church, I got to witness many individuals turn their lives over to God. I saw their drive and witnessed the zeal they manifested when they first accepted Christ! For one reason or another, as time passed, I saw that same person's drive and zeal fade away. I wondered as a child what happened to those individuals. I asked myself, "Why are they not acting the same way anymore?" Then, I got older and experienced the same thing. I realized the reason for the relapse is because we are not connecting with God on a regular basis through prayer and staying in His word.

If we are God's people, then why are we not getting intimate with Him in prayer? Why are we not immersing ourselves more in His word? Many relationships fall apart due to the lack of communication. Usually, one person is doing the communicating and trying to keep the relationship alive, while the other person is reaping the benefits and coasting along. We do the same thing to our Mighty God. Often times, we only speak to Him when we are in need or want something from Him, and that is why our prayers do not last more than two minutes. I am not saying if you pray for two minutes or less it is wrong, but there is so much to tell God that makes two minutes seem like thirty seconds. Consider taking your time and speaking to God for as long as it takes to fully express yourself to Him.

There was an individual who used to only call me when she needed some form of service from me - a ride, advice, or money. But, she never called to casually say hello or try to build a true relationship or friendship with me. One day, I just had enough and decided not to answer her call since I had already preconceived the nature of her call. The thing is, we do the same thing to God, and sometimes God does the same thing I did to that person. According to Bible Encyclopedia, prayer is "conversation with God; the intercourse of the soul with Jesus Christ, not in contemplation or meditation, but in direct address to Him." I must confess that I like the drive the Muslims have. They conduct five prayers a day. They believe in prayer; it gives them inner peace, joy, happiness, and comfort that their god is pleased with them. We all should aim to conduct prayer more than once a day.

> *Think deeply: How many times a day do you talk to someone you love?*
>
> *Now, ask yourself: How many times a day do I talk to God through His Son Jesus Christ?*

The Importance of Priority

If we believe our God (Jesus) is real and that His grace and love nourishes us every morning, then why is it such a big conundrum to pray to our Supreme Creator? This question can be answered with a simple phrase: Because we do not prioritize prayer time in our daily lives. Making prayer a priority in our lives would keep us from falling out of love with Jesus, and it will help keep the relationship alive. When you love someone, you make time for them. Your time is very precious. Therefore, when you make time to go before God in prayer, it shows how respectful and important He is in your life. King David said in the book of Psalms, "Evening, morning, and noon he cries out [in distress], and the Lord heard his voice" (55:17, NIV). Prayer helps us to find God, to hear from God, and to know Him more intimately.

It takes more than just going to church to build a healthy and intimate relationship with Jesus Christ. Spending private time with Him in prayer enables us to experience God on a personal level like no other. Prayer is so important that Jesus Christ prayed when He was here on earth. This demonstrates the importance of prayer in our walk with Him. I want to help you increase your desire for prayer and have it become second nature just like showering every day.

To help you start this wonderful and everlasting experience with God through prayer, I strongly recommend reciting the Lord's Prayer for four weeks, morning, noon and night. If you're a parent, please use it to start training your child to communicate with God. Again, the beginning can be challenging. You might be faced with many barriers such as a busy schedule and Satan, who will try to make this process impossible to accomplish. Please remember that prayer will help you change, relax, grow, reduce anxiety, and most importantly get closer with God. Furthermore, it offers an opportunity to experience Him in a unique and powerful way, which allows us to discover all the great qualities God has.

I pray that you don't fall into the trap of the enemy. Instead, I hope that you truly allow yourself to follow through on this journey. If prayer is new to you, please follow this model prayer for at least four weeks and continue to ask the Holy Spirit for assistance. This model prayer that Jesus Christ left us consists of: acknowledging God as our Father, His throne is in the third heaven, His kingdom has come through Jesus Christ and will come again, total submission to His will on earth as it is in heaven, and so much more. Basically, this model prayer covers every ingredient you need to ask God to help you develop this great relationship with the Lord. Even if you pass the beginning stage with God, you can still use this model prayer when you first wake up in the morning or while you are in your car. You can even recite it in your heart at a big meeting.

The Model Prayer

Our Father in heaven,

Hallowed be Your name.

Your kingdom come.

Your will be done

On earth as it is in heaven

Give us this day our daily bread.

And forgive our debts,

As we forgive our debtors.

And do not lead us into temptation,

But deliver us from the evil one.

For Yours is the kingdom and the power and the glory Forever. Amen

To truly help you begin this process, you must consciously be alert of where you are spending your time so you do not get distracted by the big bully (Satan). You see, talking to God requires consistency. Prayer should not be painful or boring; it should not feel like an inconvenience. Instead, it should be the most wonderful and powerful thing you experience daily with God. Most people have a plan or routine they follow such as a diet, exercise, study and many other plans, but sadly we do not have a prayer plan. To successfully achieve this short-term goal and get out of the beginning stages of your prayer life, I recommend that you set a plan and commit to it. I also encourage you to keep a log, and write down where you are spending most of your time. Here's an example of a time tracker to help you keep up with where and how you are spending your hours, minutes, and seconds. Remember, the most valuable asset one can have is time – but, time waits on no one!

Where Does All Your Time Go?

We have 24 hours in a day and 168 hours in a week. It seems we have a lot of time to do all the things we need and pray or talk to God through Jesus Christ. This time tracker is going to help you to manage your prayer time and everything else in your life better.

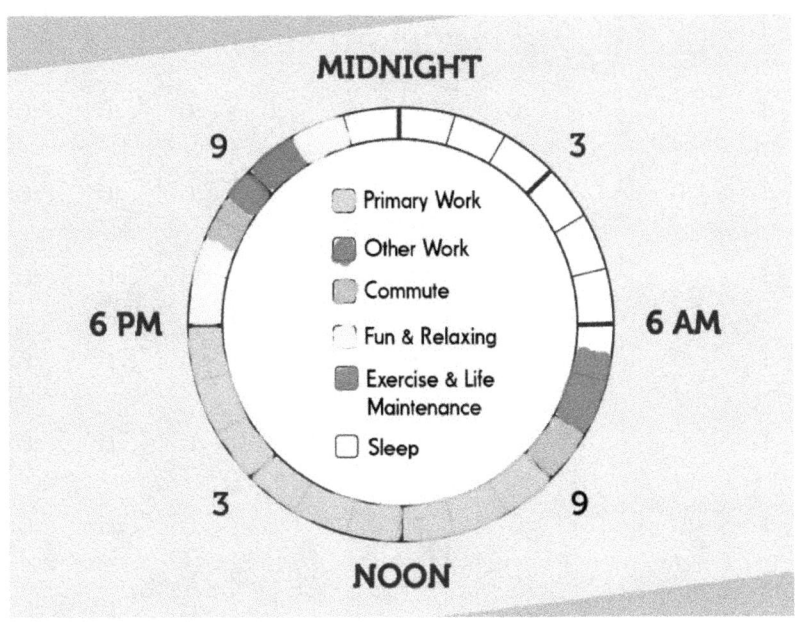

Choose Words that Sound Right

"Choosing the right words is like entering the right combination on a lock to open a safe and get to the hidden treasures inside the safe."

Words are very powerful. King David once asked the Lord to help him set a guard over his mouth and keep watch over the door of his lips. Depending on the environment, we use words that are appropriate for that particular environment. Some of us even balance it out by articulating fancier words when we are in the corporate world versus sometimes using slang words when we are with friends. In the same manner, we need to choose words that are appropriate and sound right to God's ears when we pray to Him. In the Book of Luke, Jesus gave a parable of two men who went to pray. What stood out to me was the contrast of words the men used in their prayers. Let us see which of the two men captured God's attention.

One of the men was a Pharisee who stood and prayed in the temple. His prayer went on like this: "God, I thank you that I am not like other men, an extortioner, unjust, adulterer, or even as the other man here. I fast twice a week; I give tithes of all that I possess." Now, one can say there is something wrong with his prayer since he started first by thanking God. It is a great thing to thank God when we pray for all the things we have not experienced - especially for the negative ones. However, what we need to understand when we pray is that choosing words that sound right to God is an essential key for our prayers to be answered. A better example is choosing the right words is like entering the right combination on a lock to open a safe and get to the hidden treasures inside the safe.

The Psalmist declares in Psalms 19, "Let the words of my mouth, and the meditation of my heart be acceptable in thy sight…" (v.14, KJV). You must express yourself with words and an appropriate tone that is pleasing to God. I have read the Pharisee's prayer several times, and every time I have concluded that his tone was very acerbic and loud so others could hear him. How many times have we encountered someone who is like the Pharisee - one who speaks with such arrogance, not necessarily to God, but to you and others? The same way we want people to use words that sound right to our ears is the same way God wants to hear us use words that are gentle, remorseful, fervent, uplifting, praising, interceding, supplicating, thanksgiving, worshipful, and the list goes on and on. Our prayers need to have words that are very sapid so that when God hears us, He will be pleased and quickly answer us.

Now, let us look at the second man to see if his words were tasteful, reflective, and highly favorable to God's ears and heart. This man was a tax collector. He was standing afar off and would not so much as raise his eyes to heaven. But, he was beating his breast, saying, "God, be merciful to me, a sinner!" The tax collector was the man who went home justified. In other words, God heard his prayers not only because he used the right words, but he demonstrated a humble attitude. God does not care about long speeches or big words. He is more interested in the way we approach Him when we pray to Him. God is interested in hearing the right words from us - words that show how powerful and faithful He is, and words that acknowledge His deity and glorify His Son Jesus Christ.

Articulating the right words would normally set you on the right tone. The proper tone often demonstrates humbleness and sets your prayer on the path to be accepted by God. Let us look at another prayer that had all the right words. I pondered a lot on this because this woman prayed to God before then, and I wondered why Hannah's prayer was not answered the first time. I realized that initially she did not choose the words to touch God's sensitivity. Her last prayer sounded right and got His attention. "O Lord of hosts, if You will indeed look on the affliction of Your maidservant and remember me, and not forget Your maidservant, but will give Your maidservant a male child, then I will give him to the Lord all the days of his life, and no razor shall come upon his head." The amazing thing about Hannah is she was not praying out loud; only her lips were moving as she prayed in her heart.

How many of you having been praying to God for decades about something? Maybe you've been asking Him for a child. Ask yourself if you are using similar words as Hannah used in her prayer that made God answer her. Remember, the whole purpose of this book is to help you turn your prayers into love notes so they will no longer be a struggle and can start flowing more easily. We need to use words that express our deep longing and love to God. Think of the words we use when we talk to our girlfriend, boyfriend, husband, wife, and parents. I know some of you can relate to this - especially my young adults who are in love; I mean the butterfly kind of love. You probably use words like *honey, sunshine, pumpkin, my prince, my love, babe,* or *my sweetheart.* Why can't we use those words to communicate with God? Honestly, He is our real true love, and He is the only One that will go with you when you leave this earth. Why not show Him the same affection and passion we show a human being? Here is a poem that helps us speak passionately to God.

Remarkable God!

Oh, God, remarkable God,

Your love is heaven to me

Your demeanor is ever glowing

Kiss me with Your presence

I am glad that You are my God

I rejoice in Your Son, Jesus Christ

You wait for me to change all my negative ways

Please I beg of You to draw me closer to You

You are my holy God

My treasure, my heart, my soul, my desire and everything

You are my handsome God;

I cannot compare You my love

You feed me with Your words;

You are all the protein my soul needs

You are my God forever;

You have enraptured my heart with love

I will seek You till the day I die;

I don't ever want to let You go.

Hannah's Prayer after God gave her a son

My heart rejoices in the Lord;

My horn is exalted in the Lord.

I smile at my enemies,

Because I rejoice in Your salvation.

No one is holy like the Lord,

For there is none besides You,

Nor is there any rock like our God.

Talk no more so very proudly;

Let no arrogance come from your mouth,

For the Lord is the God of knowledge; and by Him actions are weighted.

The bows of the mighty men are broken, and those who stumbled are girded with strength.

Those who were full have hired themselves out for bread, and the hungry have ceased to hunger.

Even the barren has borne seven, and she who has many children has become feeble.

The Lord kills and makes alive; He brings down to the grave and brings up.

The Lord makes poor and makes rich; He brings low and lifts up.

He raises the poor from the dust and lifts the beggar from the ash heap,

To set them among princes and make them inherit the throne of glory.

For the pillars of the earth are the Lord's, and He has set the world upon them.

> He will guard the feet of His saints, but the wicked shall be silent in darkness.
>
> For by strength no man shall prevail. The adversaries of the Lord shall be broken in pieces;
>
> From Heaven He will thunder against them.
>
> The Lord will judge the ends of the earth.
>
> He will give strength to His king,
>
> And exalt the horn of His anointed.

I encourage you to bring your prayer to life by not using fancy words unless you desire. Instead, simply try using words that will be pleasing and make God happy to move in your favor. When we first love somebody, it is not because of their actions but because of the words they use to communicate with us. Therefore, we must realize words are very powerful! If they can make us mere humans fall in love, then imagine how they can make God, who is love, be in love with us. The first chapter of the Book of John states, "In the beginning was the Word, and the Word was with God, and the Word was God." He was with God in the beginning. All things were created through Him, and apart from Him not one thing was created that has been created.

You can always ask the Holy Spirit for help if you are unable to find the right words. He will guide you on how to pray and what words to use when communicating to

God, but you must ask Him. Do not be afraid to use the Bible to assist in choosing words that sound right. I recommend using the YouVersion Bible App or visiting YouVersion.com. I am not advertising for them, but they have great resources on prayers that I find to be very useful. They even have a plan or devotional entitled "Grow Your Bible Vocabulary" by Time of Grace. Please use it along with this book.

Prayer Skills

"Your experiences with God will serve as a building block in your prayer life."

Skill is defined as "the ability to do something well; aptitude or talent." In my career, I have learned to teach a lot of skills to people of all ages. There are different types of skills such as life skills, social skills, academic skills, communication skills, and more. However, I have never read anything about prayer skills. I must vent a little... Most organizations or institutions have mentors to teach new employees the skills needed to do their jobs. Yet, in our churches, we lack mentorship to guide the converts that come to Christ. We just leave them and expect the Holy Spirit to do all the work. While He will do His part, the church, in my opinion, is to be the greatest institution equipped with the proper resources people need. Jesus Christ said in the Book of John that we are not of the world as He is not of the world (John 17:16a). In order to learn to communicate with God, we need to develop the right prayer skills.

If prayer was something that God just looked upon nonchalantly, then Jesus Christ would not have taught the disciples how to pray and leave different sample prayers for us to apply today. The Book of John shows us that when Jesus prays, He prays for Himself as well as for His disciples. The first time I read this, I asked the Holy Spirit to teach me to understand why Jesus prayed for Himself. I could not understand why He needed prayer. After all, *He is God.* The answer was very simple: God never asks us to do something that He Himself does not do. He is not like human parents who will tell their children to do what they are telling them, but do not do what they are doing. That's called hypocrisy, and that is one quality God does not have.

Jesus Christ showed us the importance of praying not just for ourselves but for others as well. Numerous times in His prayers, He included His disciples as He prayed to His father. Praying and interceding for others will keep you in God's will. It pleases Him when we think of others in our prayers. Here's the prayer Jesus prayed: "Father, the hour has come. Glorify Your Son so that the Son may glorify You, as You have given Him authority over all flesh, that He to build the vocabulary needed to pray as Jesus did."

If you're no stranger to praying, then you already have an idea of how to communicate with God. Still, there is always room for growth to build your prayer skills. Do not limit yourself and think that you have mastered it already. Your prayer skills will grow as you experience more with God. Your experiences with God will serve as a building block in your prayer life. There are many reasons Christians stop praying or talking to God. One of the reasons is that we stop asking the Holy Spirit for guidance and having the right mind to pray. Therefore, our prayer lives become stagnant. Here is my prayer for you: *Father, I pray through Your Son Jesus*

Christ, the time is near. Please use me so that I can glorify Your Son, Jesus Christ and give me the authority and dominion over all to bring other souls to your kingdom the same way you used John, Peter, Paul, Billy Graham and many more.

Six Rigorous Prayer Techniques/Skills

There might be thousands of prayer skills or techniques, but here are six techniques you can begin using right away to turn your prayers into love notes.

> ***P**: Powerful & Precise*
> ***R**: Responsibility*
> ***A**: Assertive & Adventurous*
> ***Y**: Youthful*
> ***E**: Effective*
> ***R**: Resourceful & Reverential*

1. **Put Jesus First**

Jesus said, anything we ask God in His name, He will give us. Then, He went on to say until now we have asked for nothing in His name. A lot of times, I hear people say God has not answered any of their prayers or God is not listening. I say to myself, *"Are they asking in Jesus' name when they pray?"* We must acknowledge our Savior, Jesus Christ.

2. **Reverential**

We must make sure we speak to our powerful God in a respectful way and not in a demanding tone that requires Him to do something for us or else we will no longer serve Him. We should use a reverential voice that is sweet, calm, pure, and humble.

3. **Assertive**

We need to have confidence when we pray. One way to be assertive is through Faith. "Because of Christ, and faith in Him, we can now come boldly and confidently into God's presence." (Ephesians 3:12, NLT) If we are praying and yet doubting, then we are wasting our time. I remember watching *Oprah*, and she was interviewing a rapper that goes by the name of 50 Cent. During the interview, he said something very powerful about prayer. It spoke to me during a time I was praying God about something, yet worrying at the same time. He said, "You either pray or worry. Do not do both. If you are going to pray and worry about it, how do you want God to feel about you?" Very powerful!

4. **Expressing Yourself**

When we first meet someone, we do not express ourselves fully because we do not want to be judged. Therefore, we tend to reserve our true selves. I remember getting real angry at someone, but I controlled my response. Later, when I went to God in prayer, I said, "God if You did not change me, only You know what I would have done and said to that individual. So, please, I am asking You in Jesus' name to continue to change me so I can be rid of my old self completely. Please deliver me from the devil's plan. I love You, my beloved God." Remember, God is omnipotent, omniscient, and omnipresent. He knows you. Just be your true self when you are talking to Him.

5. **Effectiveness**

Our prayers need to be effective. According to www.gotquestions.org, effective prayer is a way to strengthen our relationship with our Father in heaven. The first thing we need to understand about effective prayer is that our Lord and Savior Jesus Christ had to suffer and die on the cross to even make it possible for us to approach the throne of grace to worship and pray (Hebrews 10:19-25). When we study and obey His words and seek to please Him, the same God who made the sun stand still upon the request of Joshua (Joshua 10:12-13) invites us to come boldly before the throne of grace and pray with confidence that He will extend His mercy and grace to help us in our time of need (Hebrews 4:16). We all want our prayers to be "effective" so much so that when we focus on the "results" of our prayers, we lose sight of the incredible privilege we have to pray. Such privilege we have! The opportunity to speak to the Creator of the universe in itself is an amazing thing! Even more astounding is the fact that He hears us and acts on our behalf!

6. **Renew Your Prayer**

Do not stay in an old fashion way of praying by using repetitive words to God. You should know when it is time to spice up your prayers and change things up. Renew it by taking responsibility of when to pray, balancing your prayer by addressing God with all sorts request and supplications, and growing spiritually by studying His words.

Even if you are already a prayer warrior, still use the six prayer techniques to continue knowing how and when to communicate to God in a more loving way and not in a needing way. This should raise awareness that we need to have as many prayer skills to help us to make our prayers highly effective. Do not worry about when God is going to answer your prayers. Just know that He will answer them in His timing! Jonah did not know God was going to command the great fish to vomit him out onto dry land, but he was praying to God while he was inside the fish.

Rendezvous

"…try setting a date with God without anyone around without limiting yourself to a specific time limit and just talk to Him."

*I*t was mid-August 2013. I woke up early in the morning to pray. After my interaction with God, I stayed quiet to hear His voice, and surely, I did hear it. This was probably the third time I had heard Him speak to me orally. He said to me, "Why don't you ever spend an intimate moment with me?" That question caught me off guard, considering that I just finished spending time in prayer with Him. However, God was not satisfied with a ritual from me. He took me back to when I used to go out on dates with guys. He reminded me that when I liked them, I would agree to their requests to take me out. Then, I realized simply praying to God was not enough. From that moment, I started to set dates with God when no one was around - just our private time.

Rendezvous is a French word that means a date. Since then, it has been almost four years since I have been going out on a date with God, the Father, the Son, Jesus Christ, and the Holy Spirit. I have been setting a time and day of every month and sometimes twice a month to go into God's house by myself and spend that intimate time with Him. These have been the greatest times. I have been feeling so peaceful and calm that when I am there, I do not want to leave. I now know what King David felt when he said he loves when they ask him to go into the House of the Lord. It might sound crazy, but all God wants is for us to truly have this intimate time with

Him, and He will use things that interest us so He can get us to build a love nest with Him.

In the Book of Hosea, God took humanly lessons to demonstrate how He felt each time His people committed spiritual prostitution against Him. God is continually applying similar methods even today with us. I love the whole Book of Hosea; it has helped me to turn my prayer into love note. Moreover, it has given me a better understanding of God's love for us and how He longs for us to have intimacy with Him. God has feelings just as we do. He knows how it feels to have a broken heart, which He clearly states in Hosea. Each time we stop praying or stop coming into the house of the Lord, we are breaking God's heart the same way someone would have broken our heart. The rendezvous idea has helped me to fall in love with God and experience this mighty romance. I can't put all the chapters of the Book of Hosea here, but here is the second chapter of the book; it helps give a better idea of His feelings.

"Then you will say to your brothers, 'You are my people,' and you will say to your sisters, 'He has shown mercy to you.' "Argue with your mother. Argue with her because she is no longer my wife, and I am no longer her husband! Tell her to stop being like a prostitute. Tell her to take away her lovers[c] from between her breasts.³ If she refuses to stop her adultery, I will strip her naked and leave her like the day she was born. I will take away her people, and she will be like an empty, dry desert. I will kill her with thirst. ⁴ I will have no pity on her children because they are the children of prostitution. ⁵ Their mother has acted like a prostitute. She should be ashamed of what she did. She said, 'I will go to my lovers, who give me food and water, wool and linen, wine and olive oil.' ⁶ "So I, the Lord, will block Israel's road with thorns, and I will build a wall. Then she will not be able to find her path. ⁷ She will run after her lovers, but she will not be able to catch up with them. She will look for her lovers, but she will not be able to find them. Then she will say, 'I will go back to my husband. Life was better for me when I was with him. Life was better then than it is now.' ⁸ "Israel didn't know that I, the Lord, was the one who gave her grain, wine, and oil. I kept giving her more and more silver and gold, but she used this silver and gold to make statues of Baal. ⁹ So I will return and take back my grain at the time it is ready to be harvested. I will take back my wine at the time the grapes are ready. I will take back my wool and linen. I gave those things to her so that she could cover her naked body. ¹⁰ Now I will strip her. She will be naked, so all her lovers can see her. No one will be able to save her from my power. ¹¹ I will take away all her fun. I will stop her festivals, her New Moon celebrations, and her days of rest. I will stop all her special feasts. ¹² I will destroy her vines and fig trees. She said, 'My lovers gave these things to me.' But I will change her gardens— they will become like a wild forest. Wild animals will come and eat from those plants.

¹³ "Israel served false gods, so I will punish her. She burned incense to those false gods. She dressed up—she put on her jewelry and nose ring. Then she went to her lovers and forgot me." This is what the Lord has said. ¹⁴ "So I, the Lord, will speak romantic words to her. I will lead her into the desert and speak tender words. ¹⁵ There I will give her vineyards. I will give her Achor Valley as a doorway of hope. Then she will answer as she did when she came out of the land of Egypt." ¹⁶ This is what the Lord says. "At that time, you will call me 'My husband.' You will not call me 'My Baal.' ¹⁷ I will take the names of those false gods out of her mouth. Then people will not use those names again. ¹⁸ "At that time I will make an agreement for the Israelites with the animals of the field, the birds of the sky, and the crawling things on the ground. I will break the bow, the sword, and the weapons of war in that land. I will make the land safe, so the people of Israel can lie down in peace. ¹⁹ And I will make you my bride forever. I will make you my bride with goodness and justice and with love and mercy. ²⁰ I will make you my faithful bride. Then you will really know the Lord. ²¹ And at that time I will answer." This is what the Lord says. "I will speak to the skies, and they will give rain to the earth. ²² The earth will produce grain, wine, and oil, and they will meet Jezreel's needs. ²³ I will sow her many seeds on her land. To Lo-Ruhamah, I will show mercy. To Lo-Ammi, I will say, 'You are my people.' And they will say to me, 'You are our God.'"

We sometimes wake up late, rush to say a quick two-minute prayer, and rush out of the house. Other times, we pray continuously and still rush out of His presence. Then, when it is time for God to communicate back with us, we are nowhere to be found. How many times have you gone out on a date, did all the talking, and then left? That would be kind of rude and selfish if you acted that way. Well, most times that is exactly what we do to God. That is why most people think it is a myth if we share with someone that God speaks to us. The response to such statement is maybe we are hearing voices. However, God does speak to us in many ways. Trust me on this. Try setting a date with God without anyone around, without limiting yourself to a specific time limit, and just talk to Him. Even if you need to laugh, just do it. I guarantee God will talk to you or your spirit. He might talk to you in your heart, you might hear His sweet voice, or whichever way He chooses to communicate with you. Nonetheless, He will speak to you.

Preachers or Bible teachers often quote Jeremiah 29:11, "For I know the plans I have for you," declares the LORD, "plans to prosper you and not to harm you, plans to give you hope and a future. (NIV) I realize they often leave out, "Then, you will call on me and come and pray to me, and I will listen to you. You will seek me and find me when you seek me with all your heart." (vv. 12-13 NIV) I love the movie *War Room*. I love the demonstration Priscilla showed when she talked to God and to the devil, letting him know things have changed in her house. Every man and woman of God in the past had a place of rendezvous where they communicated with God. Moses had the mountain where he used to go up and God spoke to him from there. Hannah had her rendezvous in the temple to go and speak to the Lord.

Once you get this personal intimacy with God, then you can start thinking about conducting a group prayer with your friends or girlfriends from church instead of grouping around to gossip. It's like having a group prayer date with God. One of my best friends who lives in Orlando, FL has been driving me insane to have a double date with our spouses. In a way, it will be the same as having a group prayer meeting or a group prayer line. Find a location that's discreet and quiet. Try places like the park during certain times of day, your home or church, and many more locations you can think would be feasible to you.

Finest Prayer

"Your prayers need to be powerful, sincere and come straight from your heart…"

*A*ll prayers count. However, there is a spiritual level we should reach with God where our prayers need to be high quality and exceptional. Scripture states, "The effective, fervent prayer of the righteous man avails much." (James 5:16b, KJV) This is a big deal when it comes to making our prayers powerful. So, regardless of the circumstances or barriers, we know through prayers we will come out as victors. This chapter is intended to provide you with some of the most powerful and finest prayers for your arsenal. I encourage using these powerful prayers until you can develop your own prayer language and style to communicate with God.

To begin, there are different types of prayers such as praying for guidance, praying for a spouse, praying for children, praying for safety, etc. Regardless of the subject or need, we must connect with God on a regular basis. It is essential for us as God's people to pray and not minimize the need to converse at every level regardless of the need. Sometimes it will be God directing us to pray for something specific. For instance, in the last chapter of the Book of Job, God asked Job's friends to go to Job so he can pray for them because His wrath aroused against them. Job said his finest prayer to God for his friends, and then God accepted his prayer and restored Job's losses. (Job 42:7-10) An earnest prayer can do much to deliver your friends and family, and even have God move in your favor in ways you couldn't even imagine.

Wrap your mind around this: God loves us so much that He, Himself is asking us to pray to Him. It almost seems as if He is flattering us instead of us flattering Him. Consider all He has done for us... We should humbly seek to give Him the finest prayers from our hearts, instead of waiting for Him to seek us out. Below you will find samples of prayers that you can use daily to help you and your family of all ages pray to God through Jesus Christ. We do not want to raise a generation who lacks prayer skills and never recite a prayer to God, our Lord. As you go through some of the prayers, I would love for you to think of how amazing and powerful it will be to hear God talk back to you as you start communicating to Him daily and reciting some of these powerful prayers. Your prayers do not necessarily need to be long every day, but they need to be powerful, sincere, and straight from your heart - even if you are just reciting them.

One of the finest prayers you can practice reciting is from Abraham's servant who prayed this prayer when he went to look for a wife for Isaac. I must confess that this was one of the prayers I copied and used to pray to God for a husband, and surely God favored me. Part of this prayer comes from Exodus 15, which was the Song of Moses. Moses and the children of Israel sang this song to the Lord, and spoke, saying:

"I will pray to the Lord, for You have triumphed gloriously!

The horse and its rider You have thrown into the sea!

The Lord is my strength, my life, and song And You have become my salvation through Your Son, Jesus Christ; He is my God, and I will praise Him; I will love and exalt Him.

The Lord is a warrior; Yahweh is His name. Lord, the same way You have cast Pharaoh's chariots and his army into the sea; it is the same way You have thrown my own enemies into the biggest sea in the whole world. Lord, Your right hand is glorious in power; Your right hand, O Lord, shattered the enemy in pieces. And in the greatness of Your excellence, You have overthrown those who rose against You; by the greatness of Your arm they will be as still as a stone. Who is like You, O Lord, among the gods? Who is like You, glorious in holiness, awesome in praises, doing wonders? The Lord shall reign forever and ever. Amen."

Don't Let Your Emotions Choose. Just Pray.

Most women do not believe that God can give them their Boaz, and most men don't believe God can give them their Ruth. Sometimes, they are afraid that God will not give them the mate they desire in the shape and size that pleases them. God is the only one that knows your true Boaz or your true Rebekah. I strongly recommend praying to Him before you get married. Use this prayer if you want to marry the right person God has reserved for you. There are too many divorces happening. Parents, you also have the duty to pray for your children just as Abraham did. This is not a long prayer, but it is effective.

O Lord, God of my master Abraham, the servant prayed,

"Please give me success this day, and show kindness to my master Abraham."

I am standing here at the spring where the daughters of the men of the town are coming out to draw water. Let the girl to whom I say, please lower your water jug so that I may drink, and who responds, drink and I'll water your camels also – let her be the one You have appointed for Your servant Isaac.

By this, I will know that You have shown kindness to my master. Praise the Lord, the God of my master Abraham, who has not withheld His kindness and faithfulness from my master.

My Lord, my God, the One who has forgiven all my sins. I have acknowledged that I did not carefully trust You or do as You have always wanted me to do, and that is the reason I've had all these failures in my past relationships. I am tired of messing up or choosing without You. Help me the same way You did for Isaac. Please, my Lord, help me to find the right Boaz for me. I know You have one for me who will go all the way through with me. The same way You have favored Abraham, his servant, Ruth, Esther, my pastor's wife, Serita Jakes, and many other women who have trusted You to give them a help mate.

The man you have for me, have him bring me flowers, buy me a watch, and allow him to find favor from my favorite Deacon and my Pastor since you've given them both wisdom. By this, I will also know that You have shown me kindness as you did others before me.

Praise the Lord, my God, who has not withheld His kindness and faithfulness.

Do You Hear the Chains Falling?

Pray for God to deliver you from obstacles or troubles you are facing or will be facing. This life is full of highs and lows, but just know that God is with you if you invite Him through prayer just like David did. This prayer is emulated from 2 Samuel 22:

God, my Lord, You are my rock, my fortress, my place of safety.

You are my God, my strength, in who I will trust;

You are my shield; by the blood of Jesus Christ I am saved.

You are my hiding place, my place of safety, high in the hills.

You are the one who rescues me from all my troubles.

I am calling to You, my Lord for help and please save me from all the things I do not understand and from my enemies I know or do not know.

You are worthy to be praised!

In my distress, I will always call upon You and cry out to my God. You hear my voice regardless of where I am, and my cry enters Your ears.

You are so powerful that when You speak, the earth shakes and trembles.

Out of the brightness before You, flashes of lighting kindles and You thunder from the sky.

You reach down from above and grab me when I feel darkness and especially in my rainy days.

Even when I do wrong, You always deliver me and save me from things that seem impossible. You protect me from my enemies and from those who hate me.

When they attack or bully me in my time of trouble, you save me.

Those I have trusted have betrayed and sold me out, but You are always there to support me.

Teach me all Your ways as this world is getting crazier, so You can be pleased with me and reward me for doing your will.

Help me so I do not turn against You, my God.

I will always remember Your laws and never stop following Your precepts.

My Lord, You are faithful to those who are faithful, and You are good to those who are good. You never do wrong to those who have done no wrong.

You help those who are humble. Teach me to be humble like Your Son, Jesus Christ. Lord, You are my lamp, You, Lord; turn the darkness around me into light.

With Your help, I can conquer everything and anything. Lord, You have made me strong in battle. Jesus Christ lives forever, and I praise You, my rock.

I have many reasons to pray and praise Your mighty name.

You help me win battle after battle.

You showed Your faithful love when You sent Jesus to die for me and Your chosen people.

I love and pray to you God, in Jesus name. Amen.

Don't Fix It

Pray when facing opposition. Pray for this country in times of trial. The Book of Nehemiah has already given us the key to prayer. Why re-invent the will? If it is not broken, then do not fix it. My advice again is to use your own words or recite a prayer. God does not care about plagiarism. In fact, He made us in His image in hopes that we would be just like Him. Again, this is emulated from the book of Nehemiah 1:5:

Lord, God of heaven, O great and awesome God,

You who keep Your covenant and mercy with those who love You and observe Your commandments.

Please let Your ear be attentive and Your eyes open, that You may hear the prayer of Your servant and daughter or son, which I pray before You now, day and night, for the people of this country and this whole world, and confess the sins of the people of the United States, which we have sinned and continued to sin against You.

The world and I have sinned. We have done things that You truly dislike, but we know You love us. We have acted very corruptly against You,

Your Son Jesus Christ and the Holy Spirit, and have not kept the laws or commandments which You have commanded us in the Book of John.

You see the distress that we are in - shooting everywhere, young people locked up, all kinds of sins, and poverty covering us and our leaders having no knowledge of Your words.

Remember, I pray, the word that You commanded Your servant Billy Graham, saying,

Our Father and our God, we pray that in this period of crisis in our world that the Holy Spirit will use it to remind us of our need of Thee and our relationship with Thee, and we pray that tonight if our relationship is not right that we'll make it right through Jesus Christ our Lord who came to die on the cross because He loved us. For we ask it in His name. Amen.

Now these are Your servants and Your people, whom You have redeemed by Your great power, and by Your strong hand. O Lord, I pray, please let Your ear be attentive to the prayer of Your servant and to the prayer of Your servants who desire to fear Your name; and let Your servant prosper this day, I pray and grant me mercy in the sight of everyone. Amen.

Role Model

I enjoy reading prayers from Billy and Franklin Graham. Now, I do love to mention the name of King David, Abraham, and many others in the Bible when praying to God. However, I also love to mention names of people from my time that I believe God has favored such as my pastor, Wendell Charles, Billy Graham when watching his crusades, TD Jakes, and Charles Stanley. Here are a few prayers from some of my favorite people to help you on your journey.

Lord, remind us today that You have shown us what is good in what You require of us; to do justly, to love mercilessly, and to walk humbly with our God.

We ask that as a people, we may humble ourselves before You and seek Your will for our lives and for this great nation.

Help us in our nation to work as never before to strengthen our families and to give our children hope and a moral foundation for the future.

So may our desire be to serve You, and in so doing, serve one another.

This we pray in the name of the Father, the Son and the Holy Spirit. Amen.

Our Father and our God, we pray that we all might be conscious that Thine eye is upon us.

If God can see the sparrow fall, if He has the hairs of our head numbered, we know that He watches us, that He loves us, that He cares for us, and we're told in Thy Word that He cares for us so much that He sent His only begotten Son to the cross to die that we might find forgiveness of our sins.

We pray ... that Thy Holy Spirit will draw all men unto the Savior, for we ask it in His Name. Amen.

Franklin Graham on the National Day of Prayer – 2010

Lord, we are thankful for the abundant blessings You have bestowed on America. Our forefathers looked to You as protector, provider and the promise of hope. But we have wandered far from that firm foundation. May we repent for turning our backs on Your faithfulness. We pray that this great nation will be restored by Your forgiveness. From bondage, You grant freedom. Through Your own sacrifice, You offer salvation. From the state of despair, You offer peace. From the bounties of heaven, You have blessed—not because of our goodness—but by Your grace. You have given us freedom to worship You in spirit and in truth as Your holy Word instructs. May our lives honor You in word and deed. May our nation acknowledge that all good things come from the Father above. Amen.

Franklin Graham on the National Day of Prayer – 2010

President Abraham Lincoln proclaimed that our nation should set apart a day for national prayer to confess our sins and transgressions in sorrow, 'Yet with assured hope that genuine repentance will lead to mercy and pardon ... announced in the Holy Scriptures and proven by all history, that those nations only are blessed whose God is the Lord.' We have vainly imagined in the deceitfulness of our own hearts that all these blessings were produced by some superior wisdom and virtue of our own. We have become too self-sufficient to feel the necessity of redeeming and preserving grace; too proud to pray to the God who made us! It behooves us then to confess our national sins and to pray for clemency and forgiveness. Help us to pray earnestly for our president and leaders who govern—that they will humble themselves and seek Your guidance so that everything we do will shine the light of Your glory in a darkened world. May our prayers as a people and a nation be heard and blessed for such a time as this. We make this plea in faith, believing in the mighty name of Jesus our Lord.

Billy Graham's Prayer for the Nation

Our Father and Our God, we praise You for Your goodness to our nation, giving us blessings far beyond what we deserve.

Yet we know all is not right with America.

We deeply need a moral and spiritual renewal to help us meet the many problems we face. Convict us of sin. Help us to turn to You in repentance and faith.

Set our feet on the path of Your righteousness and peace.

We pray today for our nation's leaders.

Give them the wisdom to know what is right, and the courage to do it.

You have said, "Blessed is the nation whose God is the Lord."

May this be a new era for America, as we humble ourselves and acknowledge You alone as our Savior and Lord. This we pray in Your holy name, Amen.

The rest of the sample prayers will come from the Book of Isaiah, Jeremiah, Lamentations, Daniel, Hosea, Psalms and many more. Everyone can benefit from all these prayers - children, teenagers, young adults, husbands, wives, friends, co-workers, parents and even people who do not believe in God. The Book of Jonah talks about the men who were in the boat with Jonah. It tells of how they prayed and cried out to their gods. Once they realized Jonah was the cause of the violent wind, they found out he was Hebrew. They also learned that his God was Yahweh, the God of the heavens, who made the sea and earth. Then, they became more afraid. Before they threw him into the sea, the men prayed and called out to the Lord: "Please, Yahweh, do not let us perish because of Jonah's life, and do not charge us with innocent blood." The Lord heard their cries even though they did not initially pray to the true God. Once they realized His presence, they acknowledged Him.

Parents, we need to develop prayer warriors! We must start when they are young. So please instruct your children to start praying to God and building true love to pray to our Lord and Savior. Remember, God gives us a new commandment through His Son, Jesus Christ. He said, "Love the Lord, God will all your heart, with all your soul, and with all your mind." I pray this year and the years to come that we can have a nation that is praying and talking to the true God, Jesus Christ. Please stop this irrational thinking that God does not hear our prayers just because we do not hear from Him at the exact moment we want. FIND YOUR HIGH PLACES!

The Book of Isaiah

O Lord, I will pray You; though You were angry with me, Your anger is turned away, and You comfort me. Behold, God is my salvation, I will trust and not be afraid; for Yah, the Lord, is my strength and song; He also has become my salvation. Therefore, with joy I will draw water from the wells in salvation. You are God, who shakes the heavens, and the earth moves out of her place and You are the Holy One. I pray today that You, the Lord will give me and anyone rest from their sorrow, barriers, fear and the hard bondage. Have mercy and pity on me, Lord, I have learned to put all my trust in You and made mention that Your name is exalted. I know with all my heart, You have set a day where all of my troubles shall come to pass and You shall set Your hand again to save me. The Spirit of the Lord shall rest upon me, the Spirit of wisdom and understanding, the Spirit of counsel and might, the Spirit of knowledge and of the fear of the Lord. I pray my delight be in the fear of Your eyes, my Lord, righteousness shall be the belt of my loins, and faithfulness the belt of my waist. Not only I will pray but also praise You Lord and every morning I wake up I will also call Your name.

Lord, you are my God. I honor You and praise Your name, because You've done amazing things. The words You spoke long ago are ever true, and yet still today everything happened exactly as You said it would. And You destroyed cities that were protected by great walls.

Now they lie in ruin as a pile of rocks. Foreign palaces has been destroyed. They will never be rebuilt. That is why powerful nations will honor You. Powerful people from strong cities will fear You. You have been a safe place for the poor who is in trouble. You are like a shelter from floods and shade from the heat when powerful men attack us. They are like rain streaming down the walls that protect us from the storm. Like the heat in dry summer day, the angry shouts of foreigners brought us to our knees. But like a thick cloud that blocks the summer heat, You answered our challenge.

You lay all our challenge and trouble low to the ground, and You bring them down to the dust. Strong people and believers will glorify You; You will wipe away tears from all faces; strength to the poor comes from You, Lord. I will trust in You, Lord forever, for in Yah, the Lord, is our everlasting strength. Amen

The way of the just is uprightness; O Most Upright, You weigh the path of the just. Yes, in the way of Your judgments, O Lord, I have waited for You; the desire of my soul is for You name and for the remembrance of You. With all my soul I have desired You in the night, yes, by my spirit within me I will seek You early; for when Your judgements are in the earth, the inhabitants of the world will learn righteousness.

Let Your grace be shown to the wicked, Lord, when Your hand is lifted up, they will not see. But they see and be ashamed of their wickedness. Lord, You will establish peace not only for me but for all who put their trust in You, for You have also done all our works in us.

O Lord our God, masters besides You have had dominion over me; but by You only I make mention of Your name. O Lord, You are glorified and exalted. Lord, not only when trouble I visit You, I pour out a prayer to You every moment I have. Thank You, Lord. Amen

Prayer in Deep Distress

Woe, you destroyer never destroyed, you traitor never betrayed! When you have finished destroying, you will be destroyed. When you have finished betraying, they will betray you.

Lord, be gracious to us! We wait for You. Be our strength every morning and our salvation in times of trouble. The peoples flee at the thunderous noise; the nations scatter when You rise in Your majesty. Your spoil will be gathered as locusts are gathered; people will swarm over it like an infestation of locusts.

The Lord is exalted, for He dwells on high; He has filled us with justice and righteousness. There will be times of security for us, a storehouse of salvation, wisdom, and knowledge for this generation. The fear of the Lord is our treasure. Listen! Their warriors cry loudly in the streets; the messengers of peace weep bitterly.

For the Lord is our judge when justice is served, the Lord is our lawgiver, the Lord is our king. You will save us. Your ropes are slack; they can't hold the base of the mast or spread out the flag. Our sins and iniquities will be forgiven from this day and many more days. I pray in Jesus's name. Amen

The Book of Jeremiah

Heal me, O Lord, and I shall be healed, Save me, and I shall be saved, for You are my praise. Indeed they say to me, where is the word of the Lord? Let it come now! As for me, I have not hurried away from being a shepherd who follows You, nor have I desired the woeful day; You know what came out of my lips; it was right there before You. Do not be a terror to me, You are my hope in the day of doom. Let the enemy be ashamed who persecutes me, but do not let me be put to shame; let them be dismayed. But do not let me be dismayed. I pray that You allow me to be like a tree planted by Your waters, which spreads out its roots by the river and will not fear when heat comes, but its leaf will be green, and I will not be anxious in the year of drought, nor will cease from yielding fruit. Amen

The Book of Lamentations

Lord, You are righteous, for I rebelled against Your commandment. I pretend to love You but I don't truly love You will all my heart, my mind and soul and at times, I love pleasures, money, my lover and my friends then You.

See, O Lord, that I am in distress; my soul is troubled; my heart is overturned within me, for I have been very rebellious. Everyone can hear that I sigh, but no one can comfort me because they are not You and only You, Lord who knows my heart and sees the fight I am in inside of me.

My sighs are many, my heart is faint and troubled. Lord, please do not be far from me because You are my shield, my comforter and the Only One who can restore my life. Your purpose, Lord is not to destroy but to forgive me from all my sins and I pray that You favor me.

My Prayer

Lord, on that old rugged cross of Calvary You shed your blood and suffered agony. You were mocked, scorned and spat upon, by those who denied you were God's own Son.

But the Father had a purpose, his plain to see You arise from the tomb with great victory. You conquered death, hell and the grave, for a sinner's soul such as mine to save.

Then one day you called to me to take up my cross and follow Thee. That glorious day you cleansed my heart a brand-new life you did impart.

I thank you Lord for redeeming me; and if I had but one prayer, that prayer would be... "Lord, keep me ever yielded to Thee." -Unknown

A friend of mine from Barbados sent this to me. I am not sure the source of it, and she does not even know that God had inspired me to write this book. It titles: Look! What a simple and beautiful prayer.

When you wake up say: Jesus I love You…

When leaving the house say: Jesus comes with me…

When you feel like crying, say: Jesus hugs me…

When you feel happy say: Jesus I adore You…

When you do something, say: Jesus helps me…

When you make a mistake, say: Jesus forgives me…

When you go to sleep say: Thank You Jesus and cover me with your holy mantle.

Psalm 131 reads as follow: Lord, my heart is not haughty, nor my eyes lofty. Neither do I concern myself with great matters, nor with things too profound for me. Surely, I have calmed and quieted my soul, like a weaned child with his mother, like weaned child is my soul within me. O Israel, hope in the Lord from this time forth and forever.

Psalm 130: Out of the depths I am crying to You, O Lord; Lord, hear my voice!

Let Your ears be attentive to the voice of my supplications. If You, Lord, should mark iniquities, O Lord, who could stand? But there is forgiveness with You, that You may be feared.

I wait for the Lord, my soul waits, and in His word I do hope. My soul waits for the Lord more than those who watch for the morning. Yes, more than those who watch for the morning.

O America, hope in the Lord; for with the Lord there is mercy, and with Him is abundant redemption. And He shall redeem America and the world from all their iniquities. Amen.

Father, my friend, I am aware of my sins, and I know that I am a hypocrite. But, You still love and protect me. I appreciate all the times You protected me even when I stood in the middle of danger. I am ungrateful, and I sometimes don't realize where You took me from and how far you brought me. I appreciate you holding me close to you. I don't know what I did to deserve all that You have done for me, and I don't know what I could do to sincerely show you my gratitude. All I can do is give you a sincere thank you, and it makes my heart feel better. I appreciate you watching over my family, and I appreciate all the times you rebuked me. I appreciate you using me, and I appreciate all the times you listened to me and heard my prayers. Jesus, thank You for everything you've done for me.

(That prayer is from a young teenager who wants to remain anonymous.)

I want you to grasp this great movement that God wants to start in you and with you. The idea is not to redo the will unless you wish to do so. I simply want to encourage you to start connecting to God through prayers in a different style because He is a jealous God, and He strives to be Your lover and wants to be first. I strongly recommend you purchase *365 Days of Prayer* by Oliver Powell and *Powerful Prayers in the War Room* by Daniel B Lancaster to read along with this book to help you.

In the Book of Amos, the Lord God does nothing without revealing His counsel to His servants, the prophets. However, if we refuse to spend quality time with the Lord, how can He reveal to us His counsel, His thoughts, and His plans? We cannot blame God when we do not hear from Him. You can choose to make your prayer infectious by not just talking to God but connecting in a deeper level with Him so others can follow your footsteps.

We also have the Psalms. Now, when I use the Psalms to pray, I will change some words that do not apply to my supplication and replace them with my own words. For instance, in Psalms 51:18, I change the word Zion to *me* or to *this nation* or *my friends*. God wants us to personalize the text to fit our lives. He wants us to do whatever it takes to understand His word and to walk in His great footsteps and acknowledge Him in all our ways. If we apply the same method and follow our past biblical leaders in the Bible, we would have an even greater relationship with God.

Here's example of how we take things from the Bible and refuse to acknowledge God. The idea or concept of the Good Samaritan Law came from the Bible where the good Samaritan helped the Hebrew who got beat down and left to die. He was grateful and did not think of suing. Nowadays, people are running after money. Even if someone saves their life, they want to sue instead of being grateful. The reason for doing so is because David's struggles might not be my struggles, but God answered his prayers. Therefore, I apply the same concept and just use words that match my struggles or my sins.

This chapter is a practical guide to get you connected to God, not just when you face a struggle or barrier, but to build an intimate relationship with Jesus Christ. This book is to help you to invest yourself in serving the Lord in a loving way and praying to Him daily. If we don't start showing and teaching our children now to pray to the Lord just as the Israelites used to do with their children, then it is going to even be more challenging for the next generation to walk in prayer with God.

Your prayer does not need to be rhetoric. We can never have a perfect prayer, and that is why we depend on the Holy Spirit to intercede our prayers. Yet, we do need to pray fervently to God. We should be communicating to God every day. If not, then we should hold ourselves accountable. We need to ensure that our prayers are consistent, and we need to invest time to pray for our children, our government, our supervisors, our safety, and many more. Our forefathers used to pray to our heavenly God for this country, but now we have presidents and people who do not even acknowledge God for Who He is. Here's a prayer from our third president, Thomas Jefferson.

A Prayer for the Nation

Almighty God, Who has given us this good land for our heritage; We humbly beseech Thee that we may always prove ourselves a people mindful of Thy favor and glad to do Thy will. Bless our land with honorable ministry, sound learning, and pure manners. Save us from violence, discord, and confusion, from pride and arrogance, and from every evil way. Defend our liberties, and fashion into one united people, the multitude brought hither out of many kindreds and tongues. Endow with Thy spirit of wisdom those whom in Thy name we entrust the authority of government, that there may be justice and peace at home, and that through obedience to Thy law, we may show forth Thy praise among the nations of the earth. In time of prosperity fill our hearts with thankfulness, and in the day of trouble, suffer not our trust in Thee to fail; all of which we ask through Jesus Christ our Lord. Amen. --Washington D.C., March 4, 1801.

I do not know about you, but I am a little tired of hearing people constantly talking about how King David, Samuel, Peter and Paul used to pray God. Those individuals are no longer here, but we are. So why not make the same connection they used to make with God? They were persecuted more than we ever have been. In fact, we truly have not experienced any persecutions yet. I figured if they could pray and turn their prayers into an intimate conversation with God, what's stopping us? With all the resources at our availability, we should be more equipped to get intimate with God. Yves Carrenard states, "We all know that when friends don't see each other and don't communicate frequently, they can become emotionally separated. It is the same with you and God. If you don't keep in touch with Him, you begin to feel distant from Him as well. This is why we must pray daily." In addition, the writer states, "When you spend time with someone you respect, the character of that person rubs off on you."

Recently a friend of mine sent me this prayer. I thought it will be great to add for parents to practice with their children. Train a child in ways to connect with God so when they get older they will not depart from Him.

> Dear Heavenly Father,
>
> It's morning and I just want to say, thank You for allowing me to see another day.
>
> Thank You for the air we breathe, the food we eat, our jobs, our families and the roof over our heads. For this we give You praise, Lord!
>
> We pray that You forgive our sins. We repent Lord. We ask that You guide our footsteps, heal our bodies, mend broken hearts, take care of the needy, and protect us and our loved ones from dangers seen and unseen in this world.

Thank You for many blessings, and for keeping us covered under the Blood of Jesus.

In His precious name we pray. Amen

I pray that the blessing of the Lord be with you as you go through reading this book.

Collective Poems

"Turn your prayers into love notes…"

This chapter is filled with all kinds of poems written to God by different people and poets. According to Google, a poem is "a piece of writing that partakes of the nature of both speech and song that is nearly always rhythmical and something that arouses strong emotions because of its beauty." The purpose of this chapter is to help you to leverage your prayer in more passionate and creative ways. Many times, you write love poems to your girlfriend, boyfriend, husband, or wife. However, do you always take time to write a love poem to God? I am amazed how God has inspired me to come up with titles for each chapter in this book. Last year, my pastor asked for ten people to write a love poem to God and to stand in the sanctuary to recite. I must say that was one of the most powerful services we have had. We have had many powerful ones before, but this one was remarkable and left me with tears as I listened to people reciting their love poems to God.

Turn your prayers into love notes. Do not pray because you are in distress or you want God to do something for you. Pray to Him just because He is God, and there is no other God besides Him. King David knew how to make God move for him as he stated, "The sacrifices of God are a broken spirit, a broken and a contrite heart." When I want to speak love to God, I use Song of Solomon and again just apply my own words. Song of Solomon is so powerful that it makes my soul move. If you want to please your wife or husband, use Song of Solomon, and it will help you build great romance. The first time I read it, I thought *OMG!* God moves through romance, and I had to double check to make sure I did not mistake another book for my Bible. Now, I have gathered poems from some websites to start. All credits go out to the young people who wrote these poems.

The first poem is intended for a lover. What if the words are changed to read this poem to our Lord, Jesus Christ? The same way this person thought of writing this amazing poem for a human being she loved, we can we take the time to write romantic poems to our Jesus Christ. Again, our prayers do not need to always be centered around begging God or demanding Him to heal us or loved ones, but we can make our prayers very intimate and romantic.

Poem 1

I Love You Because

I love you because
You are honest and strong
Right here, in my arms
Is where you belong
You hold me, console me
And you are my best friend
I can't live without you
No need to pretend.

I love you because
You light up my days
Fill my heart and my soul
With your sweet loving ways

I love you because
You never pretend
And if I'm hardheaded
You all ways give in
You're so easy to love
So hard to forget

Faithful and true

Since the day that we met

I could search the world over

And still never find

A love like yours

You are one of a kind

I love you because

You are quick to forgive

Overlooking my faults

Each day that I live

So slow to anger

So quick to respond

To my loving wishers

Above and beyond

Unknown

Poem 1 (Revised)

I Love You, Jesus Because

I love You, Lord because

You are honest and strong

Right here, in my heart

Is where You belong

The same way You sit

At the right hand of God

You hold me, consoling me

And You are my true best friend

I can't live without You

No need to pretend.

I love You because

You light up my days

Fill my heart and my soul

With Your sweet loving ways

I love You because

You never pretend

You do what You say You would do

And if I'm hardheaded

You always love me

You're so easy to love

So hard to forget

Faithful and true

Since the day that we met

I could search the world over

And still never find

A love like Yours

You are one of a kind and there is no other God like You

I love You because
You are quick to forgive
You hold no grudges
Overlooking my faults
Each day that I live
So slow to anger
So quick to respond
To my loving Jesus
Above and beyond

Poem 2

Jesus, Oh Jesus

Lord of lords

King of kings

You are my majesty

You died for me

Conquered the grave

Having power and victory

In the palm of my hands

Who else could paved such righteous way

For me to meet my Father

Or accept to be tortured and butchered

All this being known but still accepting the offer

To save... not just me but humanity from sin

No one I say this again no one but You Jesus

And to the day of Your death

You stayed truthful and faithful

And for that I'm more than grateful.

You washed my hands made me brand new

In spite of all my wrong doings

You saw a lost heart and stayed true forgiving

Changing my impossible to possible

Fixing me, changing me, rearranging me, cleansing me

Here and now in front of Your throne and congregation

This dedication is for You

I thank You for what You have done and what You will do

And what You will not do

May Your will be done in my life

Use me like one

Uses music to make beautiful sounds

Make of me what You desire

I give myself away to You for

Forever and eternity

I love You Jesus, I love You so much

I don't want to only thank You

Because You are the Great I Am

But also, because You loved me first.

Poem 3

I Love You, Jesus

When I look at You, crucified on the cross,

I come face to face with the evil of sin.

When I look at You, abandoned by man,

I just want to sing to You in the best way I can.

I love You JesusI love You so much

Stay with me, don't leave me,

I want to love You until the day I die.

When I look at You, hung on the cross,

I look into Your face, I see my friend.

When I look at You, forsaken by men,

I feel sore to my bones, but forever to You in debt.

I love You, Jesus

I love You, so much

Stay with me, don't leave me,

I want to love You until my very last breath

When I look at You, in pain on the cross,

My heart misses a beat, watching You hang on a tree.

When I look at You, insulted by men,

I feel Your love inside me, a love with no end.

I love You Jesus

I love You so much

Stay with me, don't leave me,

I want to love You unto eternity.

Poem 4

Greatest Love

You bring me laughter when I'm down,

Always there to lift my frown...

You hold me tight when I'm cold,

You'll stand by me till I grow old...

Loving me like no other,

Gentle and sweet just like a mother...

Your love is pure forever true,

Inside my heart is a place for You…

The touch of Your lips against my skin,

Softness so smooth brushing along my chin...

Words of compassion forever sweet,

However was I so lucky to have meet...

My dearest love I hold so dear,

For never do I have to fear...

Honest and truthful in loving me,

Always and forever it is she...

The woman I love and have given my heart,

To live this life and never depart...

A beauty I found upon thee eye,

Captured my heart and I chose to be by...
Her side through good times and the bad,
To comfort and love her even when she's sad...
She is my life she is my love,
She is the greatest gift from up above...

Poem 4 is so beautiful that a woman must be crazy not to fall in love. This guy puts her above all. He took his precious time to write this great poem, so why we don't take time out to write to our amazing and powerful God so He can fall in love with us. I am giving the idea to you. Now, it is up to you on what you want to do. It says in Matthew 7 and 8, "Keep asking, and it will be given to you. Keep searching, and you will find. Keep knocking, and the door will be opened to you." "For everyone who asks receives, and the one who searches finds, and to the one who knocks, the door will be opened."

Poem 4 (Revised)

Jesus, You bring me laughter when I'm down,

Always there to lift my frown...

You hold me tight when I'm cold,

You'll stand by me till I grow old...

Loving me like no other,

Gentle and sweet just like a mother and father...

Your love is pure forever true,

Inside my heart is a place for You...

The touch of Your lips against my skin,

Softness so smooth brushing along my chin...

Words of compassion forever sweet,

However was I so blessing to have met...

My dearest love I hold so dear,

For never do I have to fear...

Honest and truthful in loving me,

Always and forever You are my Yahweh...

The true God I love and have given my heart,

To live this life and never depart...

A beauty I found upon thee eye,

Captured my heart and I chose to be by...

You stay with me through good times and the bad,

To comfort and love You even when

I make You sad...

Jesus is my life and my love,

I thank God for giving me You His only begotten Son at the cross

So I do not perish, but have eternal life.

You are truly the greatest gift from up above...

Poem 5

The Love of Jesus

The love of Jesus,

Baffles my mind

For it's a love like

No other I can find.

I can't understand,

The enormity of it

But, I know for me

Jesus is a perfect fit.

The love of Jesus,

Is so hard to explain

For, it's so immense

Too hard to contain.

I cannot grasp,

Its total completeness

But, I know for sure

It's full of forgiveness.

The love of Jesus,

Is hard to dispel…

For, it lives in the hearts of all who let Him dwell.

The same way you have a choice to love, marry, or not to be friends with someone is the same choice you have to start connecting with God through Jesus Christ in a deep romantic level. Jesus says, "He stands at the door and knocking, if you hear His voice and open the door then He will come in and dine with you and you with Him" (Revelation 3:20). As I mentioned in Chapter 4, set a date with Jesus Christ and dine with Him in is His words and prayers. God is waiting for you to open the door to your heart so He can start building this great relationship with you. If you want to hear His voice, you must invite Him and let Him into your heart. Set up that date night with Him, and dine in His presence. I always hear most women say they are waiting for someone with a six-pack and multiple college degrees so they can fall in love. However, God is not waiting for us to change, so He can fall in love with us. Rather, He wants us just the way we are so He can change us to be His wonderful bride.

This is CRRAAAZY

"God will take humanly things to help us understand Godly things."

I love Kirk Franklin's approach to gospel music. I love the different secular musical styles he uses to get young men and women for Jesus Christ. Jesus Christ did not care that the woman at the well was a prostitute. As a matter of fact, He used her to start the first revival. It is all about Jesus Christ, and the next generation has no time to bond with Him because some of our families are not taking the time to educate them about prayer. Train a child now so he or she will not depart from your instructions. Train yourself and your children to pray and really spend quality time with God through Jesus Christ. God will take humanly things to help us understand Godly things.

I used to love listening to Toni Braxton, Whitney Houston - God bless her soul - Celine Dion, Boyz II Men, and many more. I would not have fallen asleep without listening to one of my favorite song by Toni Braxton. I have always been a sucker for love. Now, I choose to only listen to more gospel songs. If I really need to listen to a love song then, I listen to TD Jakes. For those who did not know, the preacher can sing, too. Many of our youths listen to many secular artists more than they listen to Juanita Bynum, Yolanda Adams, Sinach and other gospel artists. We do have to meet them where they are at right now in their lives. Therefore, this chapter is similar to Chapter 6, but instead of using poems, I am using love songs and turning them into prayer. I hope you are can see the patterns. Our churches need to start giving prayer lessons so America and the world can find God amid gun violence and the distress of this world. We need to create this daily prayer dedication and enhance our relationship with Jesus Christ.

Turning Song into Prayer

In previous chapters, we see how Moses used to turn his song into prayer. We are going to see the concept of turning some of the song lyrics into prayers. The first sample is by Toni Braxton. It is such a powerful love song. As I mentioned before, years ago I had to listen to this song to fall asleep - especially when I was experiencing those butterfly loves. The craziness of being a youth but now realizing if there is someone who really means the world to me, then I realize it's Jesus Christ. The song starts with, "If you could give me one good reason why I should believe you." I do not need God to give me one good reason why I should believe He is God. He created heavens and earth, and He sent His Son Jesus Christ to die for me.

You Mean the World to Me

If you could give me one good reason why I should believe you. Believe in all the things that you tell, I would sure like to believe you. My heart wants to receive you, just make me know that you are sincere. You know I'd love for you to lead me. And follow through completely. So, won't you give me all I ask for? And if you give your very best to bring me happiness. I'll show you just how much I adore you

'Cause you mean the world to me. You are my everything. I swear the only thing that matters to me. Matters to me. Oh baby, baby, baby, baby, baby, 'cause you mean so much to me.

Now it's gonna take some workin'. But I believe you're worth it. Long as your intentions are good, so good. There is just one way to show it, and boy I hope you know it. That no one could love you like I could. Lord knows I want to trust you, and always how I'd love you. I'm not sure if love is enough, and I will not be forsaken. And I hope there's no mistakin'. So, tell me that you'll always be true.

'Cause you mean the world to me. You are my everything. I swear the only thing that matters. Matters to me. Oh baby, baby, baby, baby, baby, 'cause you mean so much to me.

There's a feeling in my heart, that I know I can't escape. So, please don't let me fall, don't let it be too late. There's a time when words are good, and they just get in the way. So, show me how you feel. Baby I'm for real. Oh, baby, baby, baby, baby, baby.

'Cause you mean the world to me. You are my everything. I swear the only thing that matters. Matters to me. Oh baby, baby, baby, baby, baby. 'Cause you mean so much to me.

Turn it to prayer & to address it to God.

You mean the World to Me

Lord, You do not need to give me one good reason why I should believe You

I know You are the Son of God who took the cross and died for my sins

I believe in all the things that You tell

You said in Isaiah so shall Your word be that goes forth from Your mouth

It shall not return to You void, but it shall accomplish what You please

And it shall prosper in the thing for which You sent it

My heart wants to receive Jesus Christ and I know You are sincere and fair

You know I would love for You to lead me to quiet waters and follow through completely

I know if I give you my very best through loving

You and prayer

You will give me all I ask for as long it is in Your will

I'll show You just how much I adore You by following Your commandments

Cause You mean the world to me

You are My everything

I swear the only thing that matters

Matters to me is to please You, Lord

This song is from the Bee Gees and it is in the 1970. It is a great song and the lyric is unique.

How Deep is Your Love

I know your eyes in the morning sun. I feel you touch me in the pouring rain. And the moment that you wander far from me, I wanna feel you in my arms again. And you come to me on a summer breeze. Keep me warm in your love and then softly leave. And it's me you need to show. How deep is your love? How deep is your love? I really need to learn

'Cause were living in a world of fools. Breaking us down, when they all should let us be. We belong to you and me. I believe in you. You know the door to my very soul. You're the light in my deepest darkest hour. You're my savior when I fall. And you may not think I care for you. When you know down inside that I really do. And it's me you need to show…

You might know how deep is your love for your

children, yourself, your husband, your wife, your friends, and your parents. But, how deep is your love for Jesus Christ? Can we truly answer this or would we ponder for even ten minutes to truly give a 100% answer? Love in action is much better than in words. God is looking for us to show actions that we love Him. If we love Jesus Christ, then why do we only go to church on Sunday or sometimes only when a New Year starts or Easter. Do we only talk to our friends, I mean our best friends, once a year? Yet, we only talk to God once a year. The sad thing is we make many excuses to why we don't go to church or talk to God. I was once that person who made millions of excuses to why I was not giving myself to Jesus Christ. You have the ball. The choice is yours to shoot to score or not shoot at all. It is the concept of showing your deep love to God who gives us oxygen daily and takes good care of us. Seek God while He may be found. Show Him how deep is your love for His Son Jesus Christ while He is near, and return to God.

Inside of You

Juanita Bynum

Have you ever felt the walls closing in. No matter where you turn it seems there's no way through. You're out of time, out of sight, out of friends. You don't know what to do. I know a place where you can turn to. Deep in your heart where no one else can go. Footsteps of love are there to guide you. Just follow his voice and you'll know. It's inside of you. A place where you can hold on.

It's inside of you. A place where you will never feel lost. It's inside of you. A love you can depend on. It's inside of you. A love that conquers all. It's inside of you. Embarrassed by mistakes don't wanna show your face. Seems like your past is killing your future. You try to block it out it just won't go away. You don't know what you're here for. I know a place where you can live free. A place where your past is just a memory. It's there deep within if you would believe. Just follow his voice and you'll know.

It's inside of you. A place where you can hold on. It's inside of you. A place where you will never feel lost. It's inside of you

A place where you can call home. It's inside of

you. Where no one loves you more. It's inside of you. I'm telling you to hold on, telling you to be strong. You will never be alone. Cause it's inside of you. Everything that you need. Is inside, of you.

Song 4

This is a song by Celine Dion entitled "I Surrender." I must admit that it is quicker for us to surrender to another human being than to surrender to God. How many times do we change ourselves for someone else? We go through hoops to please others or surrender to their demands, but find it difficult to surrender to God through prayer and reading His words. Here are the lyrics to the song. While reading, picture how God will feel if we can surrender to Him without doubting or looking back like Lot's wife did.

I Surrender

Celine Dion

There's so much life I've left to live. And this fire is burning still. When I watch you look at me, I think I could find the will. To stand for every dream, and forsake this solid ground.

And give up this fear within. Of what would happen if they ever knew. I'm in love with you

'Cause I'd surrender everything. To feel the chance to live again. I reach to you I know you can feel it too. We'd make it through. A thousand dreams I still believe. I'd make you give them all to me. I'd hold you in my arms and never let go. I surrender.

I know I can't survive, another night away from you. You're the reason I go on, and now I need to live the truth. Right now, there's no better time. From this fear I will break free. And I'll live again with love. And no, they can't take that away from me. And they will see.

'Cause I'd surrender everything. To feel the chance to live again. I reach to you. I know you can feel it too We'd make it through. A thousand dreams I still believe. I'd make you give them all to me. I'd hold you in my arms and never let go. I surrender.

Every night's getting longer. And this fire is getting stronger, babe. I'll swallow my pride and I'll be alive. Can't you hear my call. I surrender all.

I love me some Cece Winans; she is amazing. I have not met her in person, but when I see her on TV, she looks so humble with the gifts God has given her. I listen to her a lot when I want to connect with God in a deep level.

Love of My Heart
Cece Winans

Thy right hand holds all pleasures forever more. It's my desire to please you'. It's what I live for. Hearin' your words and your voice, makes me rejoice. Oh you're the one that I adore.

You're my strong tower, Mighty in power. Your spirit moves me Your touch is healing. Love of My heart My heart beat races Love of my heart You're my true oasis'. Love of my heart. My rock and fortress. Love of my heart, yeah yeah. There's no other place I'd rather be than in Your company. You are my guidin' light. You're the love of my heart. Yeah, oh- oh. You're my delight dear. Father In you I trust I will behold thy face and Righteousness. I want to be just like you, and nothin' less. You know you're simply the best. You're my deliverer, and my provider. It's your joy that pulls me through I can't live without you.

Psalm 138

I will praise You with my whole heart; before the gods I will sing praises to You.

I will worship toward Your holy temple, and praise Your name for Your lovingkindness and Your truth; for You have magnified Your word above all Your name.

In the day when I cried out, You answered me, and made me bold with strength in my soul.

All the kings of the earth shall praise You, O Lord, when they hear the words of Your mouth.

Yes, they shall sing of the ways of the Lord, for great is the glory of the Lord.

Though the Lord is on high, yet He regards the lowly; but the proud He knows from afar.

Thought I walk in the midst of trouble, You will revive me, You will stretch out Your hand against the wrath of my enemies, and Your right hand will save me.

The Lord will perfect that which concerns me; Your mercy, O Lord, endures forever,

Do not forsake the works of Your hands.

To end this chapter, here is a prayer and praise love

letter to Jesus Christ. He deserves all the glory and praises because there is no one like our Savior who is at the right hand of God.

A Prayer and Praise Love Letter

Praying and praising You, Lord are the best feeling ever, and it is even better than chocolate mousse cake and the three letter words. O Lord, King of kings, my vocabulary is not sufficient to express how much You mean to me. Yes, indeed, You are my strength, my rock, my shield, my lover, my treasure box, my sweet honeycomb. Humbly to You I turn my God who turns water into wine, who died for all my sins at the cross when the first Adam refused to die for me. I want my prayers and praises to go beyond heavens, beyond praising, loving and thanking You. I immensely express my gratefulness to You, for You are God in my life. I pray to You because You are my God, my best friend, my true love, my King, my joy, my peace, my answers, my supplier, my lover, my soul. You sent your Son, Jesus Christ to die for me. You loved me before I was put inside my mother's womb. You forgive all my sins and You give me life. I want to spend the rest of my days loving, praising and praying You, my Lord. Amen.

I love watching Iyanla Vanzant's "Fix My Life." She states that in her deepest, darkest moments, prayer got her through. Sometimes her prayer was "Help Me."

Sometimes it was "Thank You." What she has discovered in that intimate connection and communication with God will always get her through because she knows her support, her help, is just a prayer away.

The Wonder of God

"God has shown the world all His wonders and His great mystery but we are so blind to see them because of the lack of connection we have with Him."

I used to hear people say, "You can't turn a bad woman into a housewife." Being so young, I did not know what that meant until I got older and realized that statement is accurate because people cannot change people. Therefore, if we cannot turn a bad woman into a good woman, then who can? I know 100% with all my heart the answer to that question, and it is only Jesus Christ! How can God take the world's trash and turn it into treasure? My friends, my wonderful readers, that is what I call the Wonder of our Mighty God. Wonder means unexpected, unfamiliar, inexplicable. If we take the three words, then we get omnipotent, omniscient, and omnipresent.

God will do the unexpected, the unfamiliar thing, and the inexplicable just to show us His wonder. When He asks the impossible of you, you will see the wonder of God. Israel's deliverance from Egypt was a sure guarantee after God sent Moses to speak to Pharaoh. But, because He wanted to show His wonder, He hardened the heart of Pharaoh. The whole Chapter 4 of Exodus tells the story of Moses going to Egypt. Verse 21 says, "And the Lord said to Moses, when you go back to Egypt, see that you do all those wonders before Pharaoh which I have put in your hand. But, I will harden his heart, so that he will not let the people go." When you turn your prayers into love notes, then you get to see all the wonders of God.

Furthermore, the Holy Spirit will reveal to you past, present, and future wonders of the Lord.

God showed Abraham His wonder by giving him and his wife their firstborn at the age of 90 to 100 years. I recall one day, I was praying and the Holy Spirit told me to stop my prayer request and to start thanking God for being the first one to perform surgery and general anesthesia with no complications. I became tearful because I never knew God performed surgery. I was thanking God for His wonders, but I was confused. As I mentioned, before I grew up in church and I have heard many sermons. However, not once do I recall a pastor preaching or mentioning God did surgery. The Holy Spirit saw how confused I was so He led me to Genesis 2. After reading, I started to truly thank and praising God for being the first surgeon. Genesis 2 verse 21 – "And the Lord God caused a deep sleep to fall on Adam, and he slept; and He took one of his ribs, and closed up the flesh in its place. Then, the rib which the Lord God had taken from man He created a woman with it, and He brought her to the man." God was the first surgeon.

When you form an intimate relationship with God through prayer, you get to see His wonders, and the Holy Spirit will also reveal things you did not know before. One of my favorite gospel singers is Sinach. I love all her songs because she brings the wonder of God in her music. One of her songs is called "Nothing Is Impossible." God is able, indeed He is able through His Son Jesus Christ to do exceedingly, abundantly, and He is sufficient.

God has shown the world all His wonders and His great mystery, but we are so blind to see them because of the lack of connection we have with Him. Who can explain to me how Stevie Wonder, a blind man can become a songwriter, multi-instrumentalist when he became blind right after birth if it is not the wonder of Jesus Christ?

God does not require much from us, only if we acknowledge His Son, Jesus Christ. King David knew the wonders of the Lord; he has mentioned them in many of his Psalms and has acknowledged God as a king. I admire God because He is God, who alone works wonders. He does not need help and He needs no permission. Heaven is His throne and earth is His footstool. Now, who can declare such statement if it is not the true God. God made all things and He even asked us before, did not My hand make all things?

The more we pray, the more the Holy Spirit reveals to us more of God's wonders and how God is the true God. As I mentioned before, I never thought when God put Adam in a deep sleep He was performing an act of surgery. I got the inspiration because I have learned to turn my prayer into love notes. If our prayers are not so needy, then the Lord will reveal His wonders to us when we connect with Him. It is the same way - the more we communicate with someone, then the deeper we get to know that individual in a personal level. In that note, it is essential to come to God in prayer so we can learn His wonders and glorify His name for Who He is.

He's a wonder, He's a wonder, & He is a Mighty God

God has done many marvelous things, and He continues to do many more. His wondrous works, no one can compare. Even when He uses us to build things in this world, still there are no comparisons. Let's take the seven wonders of the world which are: The Citadelle Laferriere which was built by Henry Christophe, and its location is in the northern part of Haiti; the Great Pyramid of Giza; Christ the Redeemer, Rio De Janeiro, Brazil; Colossus of Rhodes; The Eiffel Tower in Paris; the Statue of Liberty in New York which was designed by Frederic Bartholdi and the London Eye. Even if we combine these, they will never mount to the wonders of our Lord, Jesus Christ. Great is the Lord, wonder is the Lord, the Lord reigns over the nations, and He sits on His holy throne.

What's in Prayer?

"There is power in prayer and all prayers need to be done faithfully and fervently so you can see the benefits."

Being a Christian and having a healthy relationship with God is vital. Here in America, we have a saying, "There's nothing free." Therefore, serving or praying God is not free as God pays all of us according to our works. Our prayers are not in vain, and we do gain a lot of great things when we connect with God. Our prayers need to be addictive. When praying to God on a consistent basis, it helps us to serve Him to the fullest. What happens at the end of a work week? We are expecting a nice paycheck, and sometimes we look forward to getting a raise from our boss. Praying with all your heart is sort of like going to work, and Jesus Christ who is our boss will then answer our prayers which is the same as expecting a paycheck.

There is a lot of power in prayer, but many of us limit God, and it seems that our prayers go unanswered. There are many advantages in prayer. When we turn our prayers into intimate conversations with God, we won't even need to ask Him for anything. He automatically gives it to us because He already knows our needs. Your prayers can create a pathway that can assist us through our spiritual journey and also be a guide to feel more at peace with yourself, life, others and with God. There is power in prayer, and all prayers need to be done faithfully and fervently so you can see the benefits.

If we ask Daniel, what did he discover in prayer, he will say that his prayers brought him God's favor, and God gave him knowledge and skills in all literature and wisdom as well as the ability to interpret visions and dreams. Daniel would also add, "Twice I faced death but through prayer I was brought out from the mouth of death and God saved me." Here's a list of the benefits and advantages when we pray:

• Prayer allows God to forgive our sinful acts through His Son Jesus Christ.

• Prayer teaches us to be obedient to God and His words.

• Prayer gives us strength and a sense of purpose.

• Prayer helps strengthen our relationship with God.

• Prayer helps us to be optimistic, more relax and calm.

• Prayer attracts God's favor.

• Prayer shows how powerful God is.

• Prayer creates a healthy relationship between you and God.

• Prayer opens many close doors and offers great opportunities.

• Prayer motivates us to fall more in love with God.

• Prayer helps us to see the will of God.

• Prayer helps us not to worry about tomorrow.

I love listening to Dr. Stanley, Charles. He shares in one of his sermons, 14 benefits of praying with God. To add to the above list, here are his 14 benefits:

1. Provides timely direction.
2. Prevents wrong decisions.
3. Eliminates worry and anxiety.
4. Produces peacefulness.
5. Invites God into our activity.
6. Produces confidence.
7. Eliminates fretting.
8. Sharpens discernment.
9. Gives us energy.
10. Prevents distractions.
11. Reminds us to act now.
12. Protects us from discouragement.
13. Opens doors of opportunity.
14. Helps us discern between busyness and fruitfulness.

Don't stop talking with God because you think your prayer has nothing in it. Prayer has everything, and it even produces faith when we talk to God through Jesus Christ. Jesus Christ was 100% human when He was here on earth, but He still asked the disciples to pray and He prayed Himself. In the Book of Mark, Jesus is in the garden or a place called Gethsemane. He went there to pray because His soul was exceedingly sorrowful because it was time for Him to be put to death for our sins. All the people who have walked with God used to pray, and we have read how they gained so much from talking to God. Therefore, we are in a time right now when we truly need to pray fervently and to start seeing all the great benefits of praying.

The Process of Intimacy

"Love is unconditional, but intimacy requires work."

The Bible tells us, "For God so loved the world, that He gave us his only son…" (John 3:16, NIV) God's love is unconditional by proof of this monumental act. I once heard a speaker say, "Love is unconditional, but intimacy requires work." That is a very powerful and true statement. The Bible commands us to love. There is no going around it, but intimacy is the climax of the relationship between two individuals. Where intimacy resides more often than not, reproduction occurs. It doesn't matter if it is a sexual relationship or just a regular friendship. If we look at intimacy in its purest form, it is the deep bond formed by two that brings them closer than just casual friendship or an organized union. Intimacy gives birth to spirit!

If we look at David and Johnathan in the Bible, their relationship transcended the basic friendship that one usually forges from casual conversation and occasional getting together. They loved each other deeply…see 1 Samuel 18:1-3 and 1 Samuel 20:16-17. That special friendship between them was forged because they spent time together. A special appreciation and respect resided deep within them for each other, which no one could touch. I mentioned that I had a friend that would only call me when she needed service or something from me. I felt that I was being used. There was never time spent together that allowed our hearts to forge a deeper intimate bond between us, because it was only convenient for her to have me in her life for when she needed me to meet a need for her. My presence in her life did not draw us closer. It was just casual, at least it was for me, but I doubt it felt that way for her.

Now, examine yourself and how we casually use God through His Son for our occasional breakthrough. I am not trying to insult anyone, but it seems like God's role in our lives is just a one-way street where He is conveniently used on an as-needed basis. I love my husband, but our relationship is deeper when we spend time together. I'm going to get a little personal here. Our love life is more alive because he caters to me, and I cater to him not only when we want sex. Prayer allows us to get to know God because we are spending time with Him. Therefore, we can cater to Him because we are in constant communication with God through His precious Son Jesus Christ and the Holy Spirit.

The more we spend time in prayer desiring to know Him and please Him, the more we see less of ourselves, and the more God will reveal Himself to us. Getting intimate means desiring to give and pleasure physically or emotionally. Getting intimate means it pleases you when you give yourself. It may sound sensual, but listen to what scripture says about a true friend: "A true friend sticks closer than a brother." This verse shows that a true friend transcends the status quo and a special bond is born out of the intimacy between two individuals with no blood ties.

God wants that relationship with us, and that is why He established prayer. He wanted that special relationship and bond to supersede the relationship He has with the casual church goer looking for that next miracle. God desired this relationship throughout the Bible with the children of Israel, and now with us through the covenant He has made with us with the blood of Jesus. There is much to say on this matter and the purpose of developing true intimacy with God through prayer. I hope that I was able to stir a fire inside of you to grow in your prayer life and to experience God like never before.

ABOUT THE AUTHOR

Widline Pierre is a proud Haitian-American millennial that embraces the opportunity to help others create the lives they desire. She is a dedicated mental health professional that knows the importance of psychological, physical, and spiritual health to one's path of peace and acceptance. Her wisdom and ambition has led her to be the lighthouse for many young girls and ladies struggling with mental illness in South Florida. Widline has a conviction centered in her faith in Christ that service to others is the key element to fulfillment in life. Focused on investing in her legacy, she desires to empower children and young adults who will eventually shape our future. Her volunteerism is consistently in the areas of helping to serve meals in soup kitchens, serving youth in career guidance, and helping ESOL students become adequately prepared for success. To reach out and empower more young Christian adults, she created a very popular South Florida online based radio show. To learn more about this incredible young servant leader, Visit

www.widlinepierre.com

or email: wpierre26@gmail.com

Bonus/ Activity Page

Bonus/ Activity Page

This is an easy to use activity workbook that will help you and everyone who is seeking to have a healthy relationship with Jesus Christ. You will learn through some of the activities to take your prayer into another level with God and also apply important spiritual skills which will help you to reflect, to listen to God more and to be successful in walk with the Lord. In addition, this is also designed to bring family together and to truly start praying and teaching our children to connect with God so when they grow older they don't depart from the words of God.

Scheduling My Prayer

Use it to write in your prayer you must do in each time you pray. Remember, Daniel used to pray three times a day to the Lord and we should strive to go beyond Daniel. I encourage parents to also use this scheduling to reflect on how many times you and your family connect with God in prayer.

Time	Mon	Tue	Wed	Thu	Fri	Sat	Sun
5- 7 A.M.							
8 - 9							
10-11							
12-2 P.M.							
3-5							
6-8							
9-11							
11-12 after 1 a.m.							

My Goals:

Setting spiritual and prayer goals are as important as setting personal or fitness goals. I did not realize two years that I had never ever set spiritual or prayer goal but every years I had a New Year resolution or a goal. My prayer goal this year is to increase my time to 2 hours a day just talking to God and to intercept for others. Furthermore, this will help you to improve your prayer and also for you to gain insights of your spiritual growth.

Complete the following activity.

My prayer goals are:

_____

_____

_____

_____

_____

_____

_____

_____

Things I must Pray for: _____

_____
_____
_____
_____
_____
_____
_____

What are three things that can prevent me from reaching my prayer goals? _____

_____
_____
_____
_____
_____
_____
_____
_____
_____

Prayer ExperiencePrayer

Write Your Very First Prayer Experience

_____

_____

_____

_____

_____

_____

_____

_____

_____

_____

Write About What Happened After Your First Prayer Experience

_____

_____

_____

_____

_____

Words/ Requests

This activity is for Family or Parents to help Your Children to start learning to Pray to God.

1-	2-
3-	4-

Challenges

Think of challenges you might face or have faced in your prayer life:

1. What is/are challenge(s) you face when praying?

   _____
   _____
   _____
   _____
   _____
   _____
   _____

2. Why you think you are facing those challenges and what are hard about them? _____

   _____
   _____
   _____
   _____
   _____
   _____

What do you plan to do so your prayer can be fervently?

_____

_____

_____

_____

_____

_____

_____

How do you intend to grow from these challenges?

_____

_____

_____

_____

_____

_____

_____

_____

_____

Love Notes/Letters

Write Your Own Love Letters To Jesus Christ

Acrostic

God – Greatness. Oxygen. Diverse
 Grace
 Original   Justice
Caring
 Deep
Erudite   Heavens
                                 Strength
              Redemption
                             Upright
              Innovative
                              Shield
                Success

                  Trust

TURNING PRAYERS INTO LOVE NOTES

Tasteful – Unique – Resourceful – Neat-Intellectual-Necessary-Grace   Powerful – Rational – Active – Youthful – Earnest – Responsible – Secure   Insightful – Noble – Trusting – Open – Lovable – Optimistic – Venturesome – Extraordinary – Nurture – Organized – Triumph – Empower – Stupendous

Topics For Discussions

1. What does it mean to turn your prayer into love notes?

2. Do you think it is possible or impossible to have an intimate relationship with Jesus Christ?

3. Are you pleased with your prayer life? If yes, share why and if no, share why

4. Do you think if Daniel was living in this century, would he have prayed three times a day?

5. Do you remember the first time you fall in love with God?

6. How was that first time and what cause you to fall in love with Him?

7. What would it take for you to re-fall in love back with God?

8. Was it God fault or your own fault that caused you to stop loving Him?

9. Were we designed to love and pray God? Why?

10. What would be your idea of becoming a prayer warrior?

11. Do you agree or disagree that in this age of time, we pray less to God than the folks in the Bible?

12. Why do people pray when some of the prayers are not answered?

13. Do you think God answers all of our prayers?

14. Think of four healthy ways you can start turning your prayer into love notes.

15. Can you inspire someone to turn his/her prayer into love notes?

16. On a scale of 1-10, how would you rate your prayer life? 1 being not good and 10 being great.

17. Is it worth praying to God even when we do not see Him?

18. What would it take to become a stronger prayer warrior?

Prayer Quotes

"When we become too glib in prayer we are most surely talking to ourselves". A.W. Tozer

"I know of no better thermometer to your spiritual temperature than this, the measure of the intensity of your prayer." Charles H. Spurgeon

"Know your Holy God intimately. When you have seen His glory, His holiness and His love-by drawing close to Him in prayer – then you can usually see through any counterfeits because you know the real thing so well."
Andrew Strom

"The prayers of God's saints strengthen the unborn generation against the desolating waves of sin and evil."
E.M. Mounds

"Prayer is simply a two-way conversation between you and God." Billy Graham

"He will regard the prayer of the destitute, and not despite their prayer." Psalms 102:17

"The most important thing a born again Christian can do is to pray." Chuck Smith

"Don't pray when you feel like it. Have an appointment with the Lord and keep it. A man is powerful on his knees." Corrie ten Boom

"We have forgotten God. We have forgotten the gracious hand, which preserved us in peace and multiplied and enriched and strengthened us, and we have vainly imagined, in the deceitfulness of our hearts, that all these blessing were produced by some superior wisdom and virtue of our own. Intoxicated with unbroken success, we have become too self-sufficient to feel the necessity of redeeming and preserving grace, too proud to pray to the God that made us." Abraham Lincoln

"A Christian who does not pray fervently is a bird without wings." W. Pierre

Rejoice always, pray continually, give thanks in all circumstances; for this is God's will for you in Christ Jesus. 1 Thessalonians 5:16-18

Then you will call on Me and come and pray to Me, and I will listen to you. Jeremiah 29:12

"Work as if you were to live a hundred years, pray as if you were to die tomorrow."
Benjamin Franklin.

"Prayer is the exercise of drawing on the grace of God."
Oswald Chambers

"Study your prayers; a great part of my time is spent getting in tune for prayer."
Robert McCheyne

"Time spent in prayer is never wasted." Francis Fenelon

"Prayer delights God's ears; it melts His heart; and opens His hand. God cannot deny a praying soul. Thomas Watson

"The best and sweetest flower of paradise God gives to His people when they are upon their knees. Prayer is the gate of heaven. Thomas Brooks

References

Carrenard, Y. (2016). Your Attitude Determines Your Altitude. http://www.xulonpress.com/bookstore/bookdetail.php?PB_ISBN=9781498487122&HC_ISBN

Charles Stanley. Benefits of Prayers. Retrieved: January 15, 2017 from https://www.intouch.org/ "Effective Prayer." Retrieved: January 15, 2017, from https://www.gotquestions.org/prayer.html.

Five Prayers from Billy Graham and Others. Retrieved from http://www.beliefnet.com/prayers/christian/gratitude/billy-grahams-prayer-for-the-nation.aspx and www.wikipedia.com

Scripture quotations marked are taken from the New King James Version. Copyright @ 1979, 1980, 1982 by Thomas Nelson, Inc. Used by permission. All rights reserved.

Scripture quotations marked are also taken from the Holy Bible, New Century Version, copyright 1987, 1988, 1991 by Word Publishing, a division of Thomas Nelson, Inc. Used by permission.

The Holy Bible, English Standard Version® (ESV®) Copyright © 2001 by Crossway, a publishing ministry of Good News Publishers. All rights reserved. ESV Text Edition: 2016

Scripture quotations are also taken from Bible

Gateway © 1995-2017, The Zondervan Corporation. All Rights Reserved. https://www.biblegateway.com

Website Resources

http://www.poemslovers.com/love_poems/i_love_you/poems/3058.html

http://www.poemslovers.com/love_poems/i_love_you/poems

https://poetrybydeborahann.wordpress.com/category/gods-love-poems/ Read more:

http://www.letssingit.com/juanita-bynum-lyrics-inside-of-youpqtccz6#ixzz4WjRZNXS9 LetsSingIt – Your favorite Music Community Celine Dion - I Surrender Lyrics | MetroLyrics

https://www.ohrd.wisc.edu/Home/Portals/0/Time%20Management%20Worksheet.doc

https://www.pinterest.com http://mashable.com/2014/04/06/wheel-of-productivity/#qa0aPXFMzEqx https://bgallen.com/writer-productivity-wheel/ www.Youtube.com www.google.com

- See more at: http://www.prayers-for-special-help.com/poems-about-jesus.html#sthash.uTFov8dw.dpuf

www.ingramcontent.com/pod-product-compliance
Lightning Source LLC
Chambersburg PA
CBHW070456100426
42743CB00010B/1643